MOSES

A Man Changed by God

Twelve
studies in
Exodus

Hazel Offner

InterVarsity Press
Downers Grove
Illinois 60515

InterVarsity Press is the book-publishing division of Inter-Varsity Christian Fellowship, a student movement active on campus at hundreds of universities, colleges and schools of nursing. For information about local and regional activities, write IVCF, 233 Langdon St., Madison, WI 53703.

Distributed in Canada through InterVarsity Press, 1875 Leslie St., Unit 10, Don Mills, Ontario M3B 2M5, Canada.

ISBN 0-87784-617-0

Printed in the United States of America

17	16	15	14	13	12	11	10	9	8	7	6	5	4	3	2	1
94	93	92	91	90	89	88	87	86	85	84	83	82	81			

Introduction

Moses knew God. And as I have walked with Moses through the pages of the book of Exodus, I have seen him model the kind of relationship with God that I want to have. Moses was not perfect. He did not have all his problems solved. It took him years to find God's will for his life. He struggled, as I often do, with feelings of inadequacy and lack of self-confidence. He questioned and doubted and cried out to God. But through the struggles he was transformed by God in character and personality until, toward the end of his life, he was granted the ultimate privilege of speaking with God "face to face."

In this series of studies we will discover together ways in which God accomplished these changes within Moses. We will compare some of the events surrounding this Old Testament character with parallel happenings in the New Testament. We will try to make personal application every step of the way. And, as we identify not only with some of the areas of Moses' perplexity and pain but also with his strong desire to know God, we will pray that God will change us, too, into more authentic reflectors of his glory.

You will notice that this guide follows the text of the Revised Standard Version of the Bible. Though it is not necessary to use this version, it may be easier. If you are using the guide in a group, you will find it helpful for everyone to use the same version. In general, it will be better to use a modern translation rather than a paraphrase or an older, archaic version.

If you plan to use this guide in a group, I highly recommend that each member have a copy of the guide and work through each study before the group meets. This is especially important because each study is designed to take sixty to ninety minutes. If you expect to complete a study in this time, *preparation before-hand is essential*. This will also allow you to spend more time on how the Scripture affects you in practical ways since the mechanics of study will have been largely dealt with beforehand. An asterisk (*) indicates which questions can be dropped in a group discussion to save time. The leader should also read the notes in the back of the guide before each study. These give some hints on how to get the most out of the group discussion.

It is best to write out your answers in a notebook to keep a record of what God is teaching you. If you are studying in a group, this can act as a reminder of what you will want to share with the group itself. You can also jot down in your notebook what the group itself is learning.

Study 1
Background of the Drama

1 Why are you studying Moses? (For example, "I need to know more about the Old Testament"; "I was looking for a guide that seems to make Scripture relevant to everyday life"; "I enjoy character studies"; "My small group chose to do it"; "I would like to become more like Moses.")

2 We often view Moses as a spiritual giant—a mighty man of God who is so far above us that his world and ours could never possibly touch each other. And certainly, God did use Moses in an incredible way. Through him the course of Israel's entire history was changed. But before God used Moses, Moses struggled and doubted both himself and God. Certainly there are aspects of his life we all can identify with.

As you begin this series of studies, spend some time with God, interacting with him as honestly as you can about what you are expecting (or not expecting) him to do in your life through this study of Moses. You may wish to ask the following questions:

Remembering that God changed Moses, in what ways do I expect God to change me through this study?

How hopeful am I that God will use these studies to make my life more effective for his glory? Explain.

Take time now to pray, telling God what your feelings are

about the study. Ask him to make any changes in your attitude in the next weeks which *he* thinks need to be made.

3 The biblical passages narrating the history of the Hebrew people leading up to their captivity in Egypt are among the most dramatic in all literature. Review the high points of this story by reading the following focal passages:

Genesis 12:1-5   Genesis 41:1-40
Genesis 15:1-6, 12-14   Genesis 42:1-6
Genesis 21:1-5   Genesis 45:1-15
Genesis 27:1—28:1   Genesis 50:22-26
Genesis 37:3-28   Exodus 1:1-7

Briefly summarize the history of Israel from Abraham until the nation came to Egypt.

4 Read Exodus 1:8-22 to see how the stage was set for Moses' entrance. How did the Israelites become slaves?

In what ways did Pharaoh try to keep the Israelites from multiplying?

How did his first two plans fail?

In Exodus 2 we will see how God used this string of events to prepare for the drama of Moses' life.

5 Before continuing in Exodus, it will be helpful to have a brief overview of the book in mind. On page 8 is a graph which depicts some of the major events of Exodus and gives an index of Israel's spiritual pilgrimmage during the book.

The book of Exodus begins with Israel as oppressed slaves in Egypt and the quiet preparation of Moses, God's deliverer. Through Moses and Aaron, God sends a series of plagues to convince Pharaoh to let his people go into the desert to serve the Lord. This confrontation culminates in Exodus 12 when all of Egypt's first-born sons die during the Passover. This represents one of Israel's spiritual high points as God's people at last go free.

After crossing the Red Sea, the Israelites wander in the desert, experiencing peaks and valleys in their trust of God. Finally, they come to Mount Sinai where the Ten Commandments are given and where they enter into a covenant with Almighty God. This

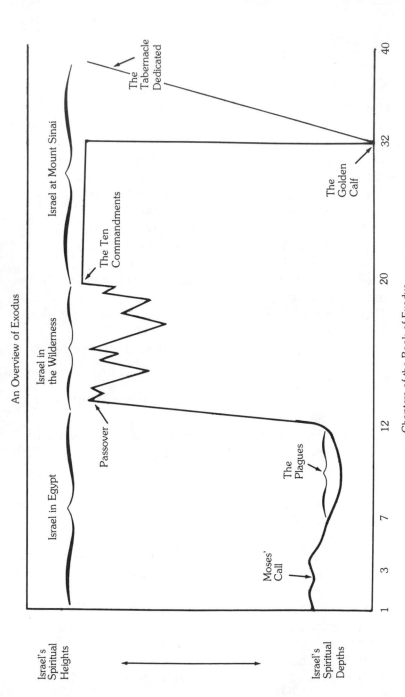

An Overview of Exodus

Israel's Spiritual Heights

Israel's Spiritual Depths

Israel in Egypt

Israel in the Wilderness

Israel at Mount Sinai

Moses' Call

The Plagues

Passover

The Ten Commandments

The Golden Calf

The Tabernacle Dedicated

Chapters of the Book of Exodus

1   3   7   12   20   32   40

was the proof that Israel had been redeemed as promised to Moses at this very mountain (Ex 3:12). The making of the covenant and the giving of the law marks the birth of Israel as a nation and is the second high point of the book.

Before the last peak Israel descends to its lowest point. With Moses on the mountain, in the very presence of God, Israel makes and worships a golden calf. Moses comes down from the mountain and in his anger shatters the stone tablets on which are written the covenant of the Lord. But Moses intercedes for the people, asking for God's forgiveness. The tabernacle is then built as God had originally instructed. The final chapter of Exodus recounts the dedication of the tabernacle and God's presence with Israel.

6 As you reflect on this study (your prayer time, the background material in Genesis and Exodus 1, the overview of the book of Exodus), answer the following. What significant facts were completely new to you?

What fresh insight into Abraham, Isaac, Jacob or Joseph did you receive?

How did God challenge you?

What else was significant to you?

7 To prepare for the next study, consider the key events or people in your life which have made you who you are today. For example, a Christian chemistry professor with an extensive counseling ministry with her students might first list such things as the time she was given a chemistry set as a child, the evenings spent tinkering in the basement with her father, and an outstanding science teacher in high school. A summer camp may have been the setting for the vital commitment she made to God, while a period of rejection and loneliness may have given her the motivation to empathize with and help others. Take an inventory of the key events and people in your life. This will prepare you to identify more completely with Moses as the events of his life start to unravel in the next studies.

Study 2
Preparation for Service

Exodus 1:22—3:1

The events of the first eighty years of Moses' life were designed and used by God to equip Moses for the monumental task God had in store for him. But to Moses, as he passed through some of these situations, God's plan must not have seemed nearly so clear. Grasping the way God's sovereignty was at work in Moses' life can give us encouragement as we view problems in our lives.

1 What were the main events in Exodus?

2 Soon after the edict recorded in 1:22 Moses was born. Read 2:1-11. What do we learn about Moses in verses 1-2?

What might Moses' parents have been feeling during these three months?

3 What actions did Moses' mother take to try to save his life? What were the results?

4 What kind of person is Moses' mother? (See also Heb 11:23.)

Assuming that God's purpose was to spare Moses' life, how did the mother's natural qualities contribute to this purpose?

Why would it be important to Moses' future leadership that he was given back to his mother? (Note especially Ex 2:11.)

5 How would the years Moses spent in Pharaoh's house have also prepared him for leadership? (See Acts 7:22.)

What potential pitfalls were there in such an atmosphere?

6 Read Exodus 2:11—3:1. After Moses became a man, why

did he leave Egypt and go to Midian?

7 Stephen says in Acts 7:23-29 that Moses was forty years old when he killed the Egyptian. He assumed his fellow Israelites knew God was delivering them by his actions. Put yourself in Moses' place as he fled from Egypt. What are your feelings?

8 What happened after Moses arrived in Midian?

9 What would Moses have learned during his time in Midian that would fit him later on for leadership in the wilderness?

*How would this training complement that which he had received already in Pharaoh's house?

10 Summarize what you have learned in Exodus 2, Acts 7:22-29 and Hebrews 11:24-26 by writing a character profile of Moses. Include Moses' assets and liabilities at the time he left Egypt and the changes which might have come about in him as a result of his time in Midian. You will be referring to this character sketch of Moses during future studies, so make it as complete as possible.

11 Think again of the events recorded in 1:22 and 2:14-15. How were these negative situations used in a positive way by God to fulfill his will for Moses and his people?

12 Think back to the key people and events in your life which you noted at the end of the last study. Did you include things which you considered as negative (such as physical defects, mixed-up relationships, inferior home background, bad choices)? If not, take a few minutes now to add to your list.

13 In what ways might God not only forgive or play down the rough edges of your past life but also use them creatively to deepen your walk with him or to fit you better for the ministry he has given you? Ask him to give you eyes to see the potential in at least one of these difficult areas of your life. What is this?

Now spend some time in prayer, focusing on this one area. Ask God to accomplish through it whatever is pleasing to him. Then thank him for doing this even though you may not see the specific benefits right now.

Study 3
The Prophet's Call

1 Have you ever had the feeling that God wanted you to do something that seemed beyond you? To lead a Bible study, perhaps, or to put a broken relationship right or to be committed to a large responsibility? One definition of a call is anything God asks you to do—whether it regards your career or a neighbor in need. Write down whatever you most strongly sense God is asking you to do right now. Keep it in the forefront of your thinking as you work through this study. If you have never sensed such a nudge from God, ask yourself if there is something of this nature that he wants you to do. Pray about it now before beginning this study.

2 Moses has been in the land of Midian for forty years. He is now eighty years old. Back in Egypt, the Pharaoh who sought to kill Moses has died. The people of Israel are praying to be released from their oppression. God, seeing their distress and hearing their prayers, takes action that begins far away in an obscure part of the wilderness in Midian.

Read Exodus 3:1-10, trying to enter into this experience with Moses as though you were there with him. What is he doing as the scene opens?

3 The wilderness of Midian was a hot, flat area devoid of trees but with sufficient vegetation to graze sheep. It lay at the foot of a mountain range which included Mount Horeb (Sinai), some-where south of Canaan. *As Moses walks along, what does he see? What does he hear? What does he smell?

4 Try to visualize Moses. What is the expression on his face, the bearing of his body, his mood and inner attitude?

5 What could Moses learn about God by the fact that the voice from the fire called him by name?

What might Moses conclude from being told not to come near and to take off his sandals?

By describing himself as "the God of your father, the God of Abraham, the God of Isaac, and the God of Jacob," what is God saying about his character?

6 *In verse 6, how do you think Moses feels?

Why do you think God dealt with Moses as he did in verses 2-6?

7 After dramatically getting Moses' attention, God then comis-sions him to go to Egypt and set the Israelites free (vv. 7-10). It is not often that we have God's will for us spelled out so explicitly What are some ways in which God speaks to people today?

8 As you read Exodus 3:11—4:17, look at Moses' four ques-tions or objections to his call and the way God answers each. Keep your own "call" in mind, too (from question 1 above).

Moses' first question in 3:11 is essentially, "How can *I* possibly do this?" What does this say about Moses' self-image?

As you think of your call, what feelings arise within you?

9 In 3:12 God's answer to Moses' first question is, "I will be with you. The sign of my presence confirming that I have sent you will be that you will later worship me in this same mountain with all the people of Israel." What will Moses need to do in order to see this sign?

Is success always a reliable test for confirming God's will? Explain.

10 Moses' second question (3:13) is "What shall I say when they ask me the name of this God who sent me?" To a Jew, a name meant someone's personality, character or inner nature. To ask for the name of God was to ask for the nature of God in its most profound aspect. Thus, God's name would suggest if he could indeed keep his promises.

What attributes of God would Moses hope for if God were to fulfill the staggering promise he has just made?

Regarding your call, how can you shift the emphasis from yourself and your limitations to God and his character?

11 In 3:14-22 God's answer to Moses' second question is, "I am Yahweh. I will be understood by the way I bring my people out of Egypt into Canaan."

Why do the Israelites need a God who is known through great deeds rather than a merely abstract, philosophical God?

In your experience, how have a person's actions helped you learn to trust (or distrust) that person?

How is the same true with God?

12 Moses' third question (4:1) is essentially, "Okay, *I* accept you for who you are. But will my people?" Why may Moses have doubted that he could get the Israelites to accept what he would say? (Recall Ex 2:14.)

As you seek to obey God in some difficult task, under what circumstances might it be desirable or necessary that others recognize that you carry God's credentials?

13 God answers Moses' third question in 4:2-9 by saying, "I'll give you three signs to convince them." List these signs.

*What is Moses feeling as he experiences these?

Sometimes Christians look for "signs" that something is God's will for them instead of simply trusting him. But there are times when God, in his wisdom, does choose to underline his will to us by giving some kind of sign. List some examples from your life.

14 Moses' last question (4:10) is, "How can I tell them all this when I express myself so poorly?" How is Moses being critical of God by asking this question?

What do you see in yourself that you feel stands in the way of what God is seeking to do through you?

15 God's response to Moses' last question (4:11-12) is, "I made your mouth! Don't you think I know what it can do?" Even in the light of this reply, what does Moses' response to God continue to be (4:14)?

16 How would you evaluate Moses' interaction with God throughout this passage?

At what point does a sense of self-distrust become sin?

17 The idea that runs throughout God's answers is that his power and presence are sufficient for any weakness that Moses has or for any problem he may face. God reassures up to a point, but then he expects faith and obedience. Once again consider your call before God. Do you feel that God needs to reassure you more or that you should move out in obedience? Why?

What can you envision as being the worst thing that could happen if you obeyed God?

Pray, relaxing in God who made and loves you.

Study 4
Failure and Discouragement

Exodus 4:27—6:13

---

1 You have obeyed God's call. You have set your course on a direction designed to bring glory to God. And then everything seems to go wrong. Has this ever happened to you? If so, how did you feel toward God?

2 God meets Moses at the burning bush and calls him to lead the Israelites out of Egypt. After strenuous objections on Moses' part and much reassurance from God, Moses starts toward Egypt. Now pick up the drama by reading 4:27-31.

In what ways would Aaron's cooperation and the people's acceptance have underlined to Moses the validity of his call?

As Moses prepares himself to visit Pharaoh, describe what he might be feeling.

3 Read Exodus 5:1-5. *What was Pharaoh's response to Moses' request?

What was his chief objection (5:2)?

Put yourself in Moses' place at this point in the narrative. Using the first person, give your feelings.

4 Read Exodus 5:6-23. Trace the effects of Moses' obedience to God. To what did it lead next (5:6-14)?

5 *How did the Israelite foremen attempt to solve the problem (5:15-16)?

What do they expect when they go to Pharaoh?

6 What was the result of their attempt?

How did the foremen react (5:20-21)?

7 How did Moses react when he heard about these events?

*How do you think he is feeling now?

8 As you read Exodus 6:1-8, center in on God's answer to the problem. In what way will he use Pharaoh's negative reaction for good?

9 On what does God base his assurance to Moses of ultimate victory over Pharaoh (6:2-4)?

10 What else moved God to take action (6:5)?

What specific things will God do for Israel (6:6-8)?

11 Verses 2-8 have been called "a window into the book of Exodus" because both the purpose and synopsis of the entire episode is found here. If you knew nothing else about God except what you discover from this passage, what would you find him to be like? List every characteristic you see.

12 Read Exodus 6:9-13. When Moses told all this to the people of Israel, how did the people react? Why?

*How did Moses react when God told him to go again to Pharaoh?

In view of what God had just said (6:1-8) and of God's previous warning (4:21), how do you account for Moses' response?

13 What was the fundamental problem of the foremen and Moses?

How can we as Christians fall into the same trap?

14 There are times when things go wrong even when we have been obedient to God. How can it seem more spiritual to stop trying at such times than to persist?

Why should it always be possible for us to thank God during apparent setbacks and to push forward unabashed?

15 In 6:9 the people did not listen to God's promises because of their broken spirit. Why do you find it difficult to trust God at times?

What can help at such times?

16 In 6:2-8 God says three times, "I am the LORD." Look back now over this whole passage. List all the ways in which an unawareness of God's true character emerges as the central problem.

17 Think about any area in your life which isn't going well (if there is one). Now look at the list of God's characteristics which you made in question 11. Using these and other attributes of God which come to mind, spend some time praising God for who he is.

Important Note for Group Study: While group members are always encouraged to prepare each study ahead of time, it is crucial that the next study (5) be done beforehand (especially question 1). Otherwise your group will not be able to complete the discussion in the allotted time.

Study 5
Growth through Adversity

Exodus 7:1—11:3

1 Have you found yourself from time to time asking "big" questions: "Why was I born? Where am I going (and why does it have to hurt so much while I'm getting there)? If God is in charge of history (and of me), why does it take him so long to right wrongs and to answer prayer?" Some of these doubts and questions probably went through Moses' mind during the events recorded in Exodus 7:1—11:3. Read through this entire passage in one sitting. It will take about twenty minutes.

2 Note the use of the word *know* (or some form of it) in the verses listed below. Note the persons who do the knowing and what is known.

Where	*Who*	*What Is Known*
7:5		
7:17		
8:10		
8:22		
9:14		
9:29-30		
10:2		

What is the one central thing that is being said to everyone?

3 In the following passages dealing with the progressive hardening of Pharaoh's heart, who does the author say does the hardening? Exodus 4:21; 7:3, 14, 22; 8:15, 19, 32; 9:7, 12, 34; 10:1, 20

For the Hebrews, God was the first cause of everything. This did not deny, however, the moral responsibility of the humans involved. It is obvious that Pharaoh was stubborn, determined to have his own way, regardless of the consequences. He found it impossible to change his pattern of thought and adjust to new ideas. In Hebrew thinking, the sovereignty of God and human free will were complementary. One means by which our hearts are hardened toward God is through our responses to the ordinary experiences of life.

4 Consider what the Egyptians, the Israelites, Moses and Pharaoh learned about God because Pharaoh's heart was hardened.

As the plagues increased in severity and number, what would *everyone* have learned about God's character?

Why would the *Egyptians* give God greater honor by watching him perform many wonders rather than just one or two? (See Ex 9:14-16; 10:1.)

The Israelites would be encountering severe trials even after leaving Egypt. How would they be helped by what they had learned here of God's character?

*What effect would the many plagues have on future Israelite generations (10:2)?

5 Consider the interaction between Moses and Pharaoh during the plagues and the effect on Moses.

In the first five plagues, who carried out the action called for by God? (See, for example, 8:16-17.)

How was this different from what happened in the last plagues?

Compare this with Exodus 4:13. What has taken place within Moses since his call at the burning bush?

6 Try to identify with Moses as he follows God's explicit orders. *How would he feel as he throws the first handful of ashes toward heaven (9:10)?

Why would his faith grow more by going through the motions himself than by allowing Aaron to do so?

7 Observe the progression of Moses' assertiveness with Pharoah in 6:12, 30; 8:25-27; 9:29-30;10:24-26. How does this contribute to the view expressed in 11:3?

8 Read again the character profile which you wrote for Moses (study 2, question 10). What changes have taken place in Moses?

How did God use adversity to bring about these changes?

9 How might God use apparent calamities to produce faith in our own lives?

Have you experienced any such situation? How did you react when you were going through the experience?

*How do you feel about that experience as you think about it in retrospect?

Are you going through any such difficult period right now? If so, how can the insight gained from this segment of Exodus be of help even before you get through?

Study 6

Vindication and Victory

Exodus 11:4—12:42

The apostle Paul indicates that to some people God's way of salvation is ridiculous (1 Cor 1:18-25). We hear people saying that if only they do the best they can, God will surely forgive them. And, anyway, how can one man's death on a cross two thousand years ago have any relevance to the here and now. Yet our salvation depends on following God's plan instead of ours. Over and over we have seen Moses obeying God even when he probably did not understand just why he was being asked to do certain things. And surely the stakes were never as high for him and the Israelites as in the events recorded in Exodus 11—12.

1 Read Exodus 11:4-10. Exactly who (and what) would be affected by this last plague?

Who would not be touched?

What would Pharaoh and the Egyptians learn as a result and what action would they take?

2 Read Exodus 12:1-20. Examine the instructions which God gives to Moses and Aaron. What was the first thing the Israelites were to do (12:3-5)?

What were they to do next (12:6-11)?

3 *For what event were all these preparations to be made (12: 12-13)?

In what way would the Israelites benefit from following the instructions?

4 *How would all subsequent generations of Israelites share in this great event (12:14-20)?

5 As you read Exodus 12:21-28, try to empathize with the "Israelite on the street." You have been living under terrific hardship in Egypt, it is true. But you have also had a home and food to eat and some kind of financial security. Your nation has lived in this land for four hundred years. Now, suddenly, you and all the rest of your people (thousands of them) are going to be leaving home, following this man Moses into the wilderness. You hear that tonight all the oldest children of the Egyptians are going to die. And you learn that your child will die, too, if you fail to carry out to the minutest detail the orders which God has given to you through Moses.

What thoughts go through your mind and what feelings do you have as you prepare to leave?

You have been particularly aware of your first-born child all day. What are you thinking and feeling?

What do you think about these instructions which have been given to you?

6 As great as the Passover promises were and as mighty as the word of the Lord was that night, what nevertheless was necessary before the promises could be fulfilled? (See also Heb 11:28.)

How do you account for the difference between the Israelites' response in 12:27-28 and in 6:9?

7 Read Exodus 12:29-42. In what ways were the Israelites finally vindicated before Pharaoh and the Egyptians?

What is the irony of 12:29 in light of 1:22?

8 Look back at this whole segment (Ex 11:4—12:42) and observe Moses. What does his going out from Pharaoh in "hot anger" (11:8) tell us about him?

9 *What thoughts may have gone through Moses' head as God gave the instructions which he was to transmit to the Israelites?

How could he have shattered all he had worked for at this point?

What character trait do we see illustrated by the fact that he did not?

10 What do we learn about Moses' administrative and leadership skills in obeying God's commands?

11 Read 5:2 and then 12:31-32. If you were Moses, how would you feel as you heard Pharaoh cry out these words in chapter 12?

How have you experienced God's faithfulness that enables you to identify with Moses' response?

12 Many years later there came One who presided over another Passover feast. Read about this Passover in Matthew 26: 26-29. To what event immediately following the feast do Jesus' words point?

In the cross we have a key to understanding the first Passover which Moses did not have. List some of the ways in which the first Passover looks forward to Christ's death and resurrection. (See also Jn 1:29; 1 Cor 5:7; 1 Pet 1:19-20.)

13 We have noted the way in which the promises of the first Passover were fulfilled (see question 6 above). In similar fashion today God's offer of salvation depends on each individual's response. Have you followed God's "directives" for salvation? What is the response of your heart to this whole study as you stand on the other side of the cross from Moses?

14 *Read John 1:11-12; 3:16 and Romans 3:25. Based on your understanding of these passages, how would you explain to an unbeliever what God's instructions are for being released from the bondage of sin?

*Who do you know that needs these instructions? How could you creatively and lovingly share them this week?

Study 7
Leadership under Duress

Exodus 14:1—15:21

Here is a ringing affirmation of the greatness of God and of his triumph over the Egyptians and all the gods of Egypt! It is also an overwhelming vindication of Moses' steadfastness before him—and of ours, too, as we cooperate with his power.

1 Read Exodus 14:1-4. What were the first steps in God's plan to bring about the final humiliation of Egypt?

Toward what end or purpose was God moving?

Think of yourself as a director about to produce a play based on the scenes from Exodus 14:5—15:21. Think, feel, see, hear, smell with the people involved! There will be questions with each scene to help you.

2 *Scene One: Egypt's Vindictiveness and Israel's Vulnerability.* Read Exodus 14:5-8. How did God use the natural feelings and circumstances of the people in this passage to begin the action?

3 Try to empathize with the Israelites as the events described in verse 10 begin. As a director, how would you convey their desperate feelings to the audience?

Why do you think the Israelites were in such great fear when God had just demonstrated his faithfulness so vividly in the preceding events in Egypt?

4 Picture Moses. What was his answer to the Israelites?

*What mixture of feelings do you suppose he is experiencing?

5 Contrast verses 14 and 15. What important aspect of leadership is highlighted by this?

In what way might Moses' "aloneness" have contributed to his spiritual growth?

6 What does God say will happen when Moses obeys the instructions given in verse 16?

7 *Scene Two: God's Victory.* Read Exodus 14:19-31. As night falls, the angel of the Lord moves in the cloud to go behind the Israelites rather than in front. Therefore, the cloud and the darkness hide Israel from the Egyptians. Moses lifts his rod over the sea and a strong east wind begins to blow.

Picture Moses as every eye is on him. What is at stake in this scene?

8 All night long the wind blows, and all night long the two armies do not come near each other. When daylight breaks, the order is given for Israel to move.

As you direct this scene, how will you depict the first steps taken by the Israelites as they step into the path God made in the sea?

How would you direct the Israelites still on the bank watching?

How would you depict the entire throng as it walks on the dry land and looks back to see the Egyptian army in pursuit?

As the waters come over the Egyptians?

What range of feelings has each Israelite experienced since the Egyptian army was first seen overtaking them (14:10-31)?

9 Recall that in verses 4 and 18, God told Moses that he will get glory. *Glory* means something external, that can be seen, that brings fame, honor and recognition. At this point in the narrative, how has God's prophecy come true?

10 Read once again the promises which God made to Moses which are recorded in Exodus 6:2-8. Contrast the reaction of the Israelites in 6:9 to that of 14:31. What made the difference?

11 Recall the name of God given to Moses in 3:14. (See question 10 in study 3.) In what way has the character of God portrayed in this name been illustrated?

12 *Scene Three: Celebration of Victory.* This scene is filled with praise. There is amazement and incredulous joy on every face. Some stand awestruck, looking at the bodies of the dead Egyptians. Others are lifting hands toward heaven. Still others embrace one another. All look from time to time toward Moses. Then the whole company bursts into joyous song! Moses sings with the rest and his face shines with a mixture of faith, joy and wonder. God has triumphed! The ecstacy of this unique moment is too great to sit still. Miriam seizes a tambourine, and she and all the other women begin to dance.

Read Exodus 15:1-21. What are all the ways in which the character of God is described?

13 Praise God using the characteristics you have just listed. Thank him that because he is unchangeable, he is the same God for you that he was to Israel.

Study 8
Life in Relationship

Exodus 19:1—20:20

1 Has a person close to you ever betrayed you in some way, large or small? It may have been a dear friend, your husband or wife, your child, a Christian whose leadership you respected. Perhaps the person said untrue things about you to others. Perhaps the friend allowed anger to build up toward you for weeks or months until a certain coolness developed between you. Or maybe something of yours was missing one day and the only person who could possibly have been responsible was your loved one. What was the situation, if any, in your case?

If any of these things has ever happened to you, how did it affect the relationship between you and the one you loved?

Keep this situation in mind as you work through this study.

2 *The Covenant is Offered and Accepted.* After the triumph of the Red Sea crossing, the Israelites, with Moses in the lead, set out for Mount Sinai. They experienced crises of thirst, hunger and war on the way (Ex 16—18). With each crisis they doubted Moses and with each crisis their doubt was met by God who met all their needs. Finally, three months after Israel left Egypt, the promise which God had made to Moses at the burning bush (Ex 3:12) was fulfilled. Israel did indeed arrive at the mountain of God.

Up to this point Israel had been held together spiritually by the terms given to Abraham and binding on all his descendants. At Sinai they were to be forged into a nation as they came under the detailed covenant of the Law.

Read Exodus 19:1-8. What does God remind the Israelites of in verse 4?

Consider your relationship with your parents. Why is it usually easier to please them in the context of a relationship rather than in response to a list of rules?

How might God's reminders (v. 4) motivate Israel to *keep* the terms of the covenant once the covenant was given?

3 Observe the terms of the covenant. What condition was Israel to meet (19:5)?

What would be the result if Israel kept its part of the pact (19:5-6)?

4 How do verses 4-6 suggest that the arrangement was to be more than a legal partnership? (See also Ex 6:7.)

5 *What was the people's response to God's invitation?

*What was Moses' role in this episode?

6 *The Two Parties Meet to Make the Covenant.* Read Exodus 19:9-25. What is significant about God saying that *he* would "come down" to the people (19:9, 11)?

7 How were the people to prepare themselves for God's coming?

What would they learn about their relationship with God from these instructions? (See also Lev 11:44-45.)

8 List all the sights and sounds described in verses 16-25.

What were the people's reactions to these sights and sounds (19:16)?

How would all this have underlined God's instructions discussed above?

9 Inasmuch as it was *this* kind of God who desired a personal relationship with the people, why would it be necessary for a set of laws to be given to Israel?

10 *What further motivation to keep the law would Israel derive from the sights and sounds and all these instructions?

The stage is now set for a glorious covenant to be established —a covenant based on the relationship between God and the nation of Israel.

11 *The Terms of the Covenant Are Summarized.* Read Exodus 20:1-20. Why are the Ten Commandments given at this juncture in Israel's history instead of while Israel was still in Egypt?

What, then, is the place of the Law in relation to salvation? (See also Gen 15:6 and Gal 3:6-14.)

12 How does verse 2 act as an introduction to the Ten Commandments?

How does this give greater meaning to the first commandment (20:3)?

What would be the difference in the third, fourth and fifth commandments if the words "your God" were omitted (19:7, 10, 12)?

13 As great as Moses and the covenant were, both would be superseded one day when Jesus Christ would mediate a new covenant between God and his people. (See Heb 3:3 and 8:6.) This new covenant would be written on the heart, and rather than being only a corporate relationship between God and the nation of Israel, it would also be based on the relationship between God and the individual.

Read Hebrews 12:18-24 noting the contrasts between the giving of the Law (12:18-21) and the picture of the Christian's experience under the new covenant (12:22-24). What mood is suggested by each of these events?

14 Considering God as the Master Teacher, why was it necessary for him to show the awesome side of his character before revealing himself more fully in Jesus Christ?

On the other hand, how do the Ten Commandments illustrate God's consistent nature in both the Old and New Testaments?

15 In the light of this understanding of the Ten Commandments, think back to the situation you noted in question 1. Was your first reaction that your loved one had broken a commandment? If not, what was your reaction?

*To put things right, what more did you want him or her to do than just clinically admit guilt?

*When you forgave him or her, what happened to your relation ship which involved more than a mere "canceling of the penalty" or "wiping the slate clean"?

16 Viewing the Christian life as a relationship with Jesus Christ, how does sin become more than just breaking the rule?

*How does repentance differ from merely admitting guilt?

*And how will forgiveness involve more than the canceling of a penalty?

17 How will a consciousness of a life in relationship with a holy and loving God affect the things you do and think this week?

Study 9

Moses the Mediator

Exodus 24

Did you ever stop to think that although Moses knew God well, he did not understand some of God's ultimate purposes as well as you do? God has made a glorious new covenant with us since the time of Moses which gives us this greater insight.

The Mosaic covenant was initially given and accepted informally. In Exodus 24 we will see how it was sealed formally.

1 Read Exodus 24. How did the instructions given to Aaron, his sons and the seventy elders differ from those given to Moses?

What does this say about God's attitude toward Moses?

2 An ancient covenant involved first a public recital, then the acceptance of its terms, and after that a writing down of those terms. These three steps are seen in verses 3-4. What did Moses do after he built the altar and the twelve pillars representing Israel's twelve tribes (24:5-6)?

Blood is common to most forms of covenant, for example, "blood brothers" are made by allowing the blood from two persons to flow into each other. See also Abraham's covenant in Genesis 15. No explanation of the covenant ritual is given here.

3 From verses 1-8, list the actions that underline the corporate character of the people of God as opposed to God making a covenant with each individual.

4 Verse 9 continues the narrative begun in verses 1-2. How is God's attitude toward Moses developed more fully in verses 9-18? (Recall 24:2.)

5 *Who accompanied Moses up the mountain?

*In Moses' absence, who was left in charge of the seventy elders (24:13-14)?

6 What symbols of God's presence ("glory") are on the mount (24:16-17)?

Why was it important that Israel still have a visible reminder of God (24:18) even though Moses was gone?

7 How does verse 18 constitute a climax in both the life and character of Moses?

8 Read Hebrews 8:7 and 10:1-4. Why, despite Moses' favor with God and the greatness of the Mosaic covenant, was it necessary for this first covenant to be replaced by something better?

Using the following New Testament references to guide you, consider some of the differences and similarities between the Mosaic covenant and the new covenant in Jesus Christ.

9 Compare the phrase "blood of the covenant" in Exodus 24:8 with Matthew 26:26-28 and 1 Corinthians 11:23-26. Whose blood was involved each time?

10 Read Hebrews 3:1-6; 9:15-20 and 10:12. Who mediated the new covenant? Why was this person more qualified than Moses?

11 Read Hebrews 10:11-18. What advantages are there for us in Christ's sacrifice not found in Mosaic sacrifices?

12 We have seen that the Mosaic covenant was made with the whole people of Israel, that is, it was *corporate*. In what ways is the new covenant also a corporate relationship between God and believers? (See also 1 Cor 12:12-26.)

What practical difference does this make in your attitude toward other Christians, such as those who seem to have a greater ministry than you, or those who have been overcome by some sin or those who are grieving?

13 In what way is the new covenant personal?

How does this increase both the blessings and the responsibilities for Christians? (See 2 Cor 3:1-6.)

14 Thank God for your increased awareness of the blessings which are yours in Jesus Christ. Ask him to make you alert to new ways to obey him because of this increased understanding.

Study 10
Fall and Restoration

Exodus 32

1 Have you ever heard yourself saying all the right things about the reality of God in your life but at the same time you were acting as though the world at hand was all that mattered? What was it like?

On first reading, Exodus 32 may seem surprising. But as we think about it in light of our own weaknesses and temptations, perhaps we are not as different from Israel as we thought.

2 In Exodus 19 God gives Moses the Law. The Law is then proclaimed orally to the people in Exodus 20—23. Moses comes down from the mountain and serves as mediator between God and Israel as the covenant is made. Moses, Aaron and seventy elders then go part way up the mountain and ceremoniously ratify the covenant in a meal with God. The elders and Aaron go back down to the valley after Moses delegates his judicial authority to Aaron and Hur. Moses, however, continues up the mountain where he disappears for forty days. Joshua goes along but not into the cloud where God is.

During these forty days God writes the covenant (probably in abbreviated form) on the tablets of stone. He also gives Moses detailed instructions (Ex 26—31) on how to build the tabernacle in which God will uniquely dwell and show his presence to the Israelites for many years to come. Exodus 31:18 completes the narrative concerning God's work with Moses on the mountain. Meanwhile, in the valley, the Israelites grow restive.

Read Exodus 32:1-20. What is the immediate reason given for the Israelites' dissatisfaction?

What does this suggest about their concept of God?

3 What did the people demand of Aaron and how did he respond?

What kinds of thoughts might have been going through Aaron's mind during this period?

4 The calf almost certainly represents Baal, one of Egypt's gods. It is likely that, even during their four hundred years in Egypt, Israel had been corrupted by cults and other religions. This episode would be a case of reverting to such practices after the stern demands of Sinai. How was Aaron's compromise of mixing a feast to the Lord with Baal worship (32:5-6) even worse than open apostasy to Baal?

Note that scarcely more than a month had passed since the events recorded in Exodus 24.

5 *As the revelry accelerated in the valley, contrast the atmosphere on the mountain top (see 24:1-18).

*How was Moses' mood interrupted (32:7-10)?

6 What specifically kindled God's anger against the people?

What does God say he will do?

Note the *anthropopathism,* that is, the describing of God's feelings in human terms so that they will be more comprehensible to us.

7 What was Moses' response?

On what did he base his plea to God?

How does he argue from God's act of bringing Israel out of Egypt?

8 As Moses came into the camp and saw the revelry, what did he do?

What is the significance of each action?

9 Contrast Moses' responses in verses 12 and 19.

What do you suppose made the difference?

10 Read Exodus 32:21-35. *Observe the interaction between Moses and Aaron (32:21-24). *What does Moses' question imply?

*How, in his answer, does Aaron attempt to cover up?

11 To "break loose" (32:25) means to become ungovernable or to cast off restraint. When Moses saw that the people had become ungovernable, what did he do? With what response?

12 *How was Moses' order in verse 27 a test of commitment for the Levites? (See also Lk 12:51-53.)

*What blessing for the Levites resulted from their action? (See also Num 1:50-53.)

13 How is Moses' intercession in verses 31-32 even stronger than the one he made in verses 12-13?

What does this reveal about Moses' relationship with God?

14 As you look back over the entire chapter, what adjectives would you use to describe Moses?

Compare the Moses who emerges from this account with the one described in Exodus 4:12-16.

What accounts for the change?

15 As we Christians are aware of the potential idol of the visible world in our own lives, what practical things can we do to guard the reality of the invisible God?

16 What do you learn about Moses' prayer life from this chapter?

What aspects do you need to emulate? For instance, how do you usually intercede for specific Christian friends? How do you pray for the universal church?

On what grounds can you, like Moses, make your appeal to God?

17 If intercession is not a part of your prayer life, what steps will you need to take to be sure it is from now on? List these.

Literally, put yourself on the line. Put your initials by each item you listed which you firmly resolve before God to carry out.

Study 11

Show Me Thy Glory

Exodus 33

1 When you have given a situation to God in prayer, do you always accept what happens as God's will?

Do you feel that there is ever a time when you should *not* accept something as his will? Explain.

2 Read Exodus 33:1-11. Instead of leading Israel himself, how does God say he will guide Israel?

In what way is this also a protection for Israel? (Compare 33:3 with 19:12.)

How is this decision commensurate with the seriousness of Israel's sin?

3 *Why did the Israelites take off their ornaments to show their mourning?

*Compare 32:2-4 with 35:22 to see two ways in which material things were used by the Israelites. What makes the difference in whether material goods bring honor or dishonor to God?

4 Summarize Israel's worship at this time, as described in verses 7-11.

Why did Moses pitch the tent outside the camp?

What would Moses' role have meant to him?

5 Read Exodus 33:12-23. As Moses contemplates obeying God's previous command (33:12), what is his primary concern?

What does Moses' request in verses 12-13 indicate about his

attitude toward himself as a leader?

What did Moses see as the chief distinctiveness of Israel (33:16)?

6 In your own words, what is God's reason for saying yes to Moses' request (33:17)?

7 Why was Moses dissatisfied with God's response and why did he also ask to see God's glory?

What does Moses' desire indicate about his understanding of God?

Why would this particular request delight God?

8 To what degree does God go along with Moses' request to see God's glory?

*What does God say he will not reveal?

*What does this refusal show us about God?

9 How would you characterize the way Moses talks with God throughout this passage?

What would Moses have missed if he had not persisted?

What do we learn about how God answers prayer from this dialog?

10 How do you show that you want to get to know God better?

How much do you persist with him in prayer until he reveals himself to you in some deeper way?

11 How do you show your concern for the people of God (the church)?

How would you compare your concern for God's people with Moses'?

12 Ask God to teach you how to be so absorbed by him and his purposes that you will know when and how to persist in prayer.

Study 12

God's Shining Witness

Exodus 34

1 All of us wish that we could communicate God with such certainty and authority that the lives of others would be touched deeply because of us. Exodus 34 is a model of how we can reflect God's spirit more to those around us. Read the whole chapter.

What directives did God give to Moses concerning the rewriting of the Law (34:1-7; see also 19:12-13)?

What would be God's role?

2 Verses 6 and 7 are regarded by Jewish scholars as containing the essential attributes of Yahweh. Compare these verses with Exodus 3:14. What changes have taken place within Moses which make it possible for God now to give Moses this more detailed description of himself?

How does this self-revelation of God take on an even deeper meaning because it is set in the context of Israel's sin (Ex 32—33)?

3 Into what two contrasting categories can you place the attributes mentioned in verses 6-7?

How should these complementary aspects influence the ways in which we come into God's presence?

Give a descriptive title to God based on these aspects of his character (such as, The Merciful Judge).

4 If we want to be effective for God, the first step is to spend time with him as Moses did. In this context, think of the person you most love and enjoy being with. What do you do, what sacrifices do you make, to spend quality time with this person?

What kind of time do you spend with God?

How can you make your time with God equal in quality to the time you spend with the person you enjoy being with most?

5 What was Moses' immediate response to God's revelation of himself?

What requests did he then make of God?

How could Moses' spontaneous response to God be a pattern for us today?

6 In verses 10-26 God renews the covenant he made with Israel through Moses, though it is not reiterated fully. It assumes the giving of the Ten Commandments and centers on the festivals that Israel is to keep each year to maintain an awareness of God's presence.

What happened as Moses came down from the mountain to the Israelites (34:29)?

How would you characterize Moses at this point?

In what way had his request in Exodus 33:18 been granted?

7 Look back over the character profile of Moses which you wrote at the beginning of these studies (study 2, question 10). List a couple of main differences in the Moses you see here at the end of the book.

How can you account for the changes you have selected?

8 What effect did Moses' physical appearance have on the Israelites?

In your own words, give the reason for this impact.

What encouragement can you take from the fact that Moses was oblivious to the impact which he was making on others?

9 If I, like Moses, encounter the greatness of God in a deep personal way, I will have a powerful witness to those around me whether I am aware of it or not. As you come to the close of these studies, prayerfully ask yourself the following questions:

How much do I desire to know God? What sin, if any, do I need to confess to God or what restitution, if any, do I need to make to another? What task in partnership with God does he want me to do? Might he be asking that I take a long period of time (perhaps several hours or a whole day) just to be with him?

What steps will you take to obey any new thing God has given you to do through these studies?

Ask God to remind you regularly of your commitment and to give you his power and presence as you seek to obey what he has directed.

Leader's Notes

These studies in Exodus on the life of Moses are highly personal —some may even feel they are too personal. But only as we allow God to touch us where we live will Bible study become meaningful. Only then will the words spring alive from the page.

For this reason, it is very important that you, the leader, have met God in the passage you are to lead. As you are open to the Holy Spirit, allowing him to use his Word as a searchlight on your heart, you will effectively lead others to the same Lord. Therefore, pray that God will, through each study, work within you to make *you* more like Jesus Christ and know that he is far more interested in doing this than you are!

God is interested in doing the same in the people you will be studying with. The group is not *your* group, after all. It is God's group, and it is the group's. Your role is that of a facilitator of discussion rather than a teacher of facts. With a commitment to the Word of God and to helping others, your task is to guide the group to discover the truths in the Bible for themselves. That means you need to know your material well. You need to know where to lead them. Yet you will see that when people begin to discover Bible truths for themselves, excitement sets in which is followed by motivation. Your job then gets easier and easier as they begin to dig into the Word more and more with less direction from you.

How can you become a facilitator? *Pray.* Ask for the Spirit's illumination. God wants us to understand all of his Word, so you can confidently pray in his will. He also wants your group members to know him and his Word. Pray that God will help you be a facilitator, one who helps others grow in their own relationship with God.

Study. First, move through the study yourself, noting the introductory material. You should read through and take notes on the passage before you look at the questions in the guide, trying to understand it on your own first. A good rule of thumb is at least two hours of preparation for each study. As you study, allow God to change *you.* Only as you are touched by him can your leadership touch others.

Next, *prepare to lead.* Only now should you read through the leader's notes for the study you are working on. These are intended to warn you of potential problems in group discussion and to give you hints on how to bring out the essence of the passage. It is here too that you should take a close look at the purposes listed at the beginning of each section of the leader's notes. These are not necessarily meant to be read to your group. Rather these summarize what your group should take away with them. Now consider how each of the questions contributes toward accomplishing these goals.

You will note that each study contains some observation questions (What does the passage say?), some interpretation questions (What does the passage mean?) and some application questions (What are we going to do about this?). Don't be frustrated with the observation questions. If we are to interpret correctly, we must have a firm grasp of the content. This simply takes time and effort. Likewise, correct application requires correct interpretation. The interpretation questions could be the most interesting because they are discussion questions.

Application questions might not elicit as much discussion because people can be threatened if there are faults or problems that could be mentioned. And we all fear self-exposure! Be sensitive to such feelings while helping the group make specific application to their lives. The point of Bible study, after all, is that our lives be changed because we know God better.

A fourth type of question is used in this guide: approach questions. Most studies begin with one, two or three such questions which are asked *before* the passage is read. These are important questions and I urge you not to skip them. Their intent is to help the group warm up to the topic. No matter how well a group may know each other or how comfortable they may be with each other, there is always a stiffness that needs to be overcome before people will begin to talk openly. Observation questions are not very good for overcoming this.

Approach questions also get people thinking along the lines of the topic under discussion. Most people will have lots of different things going on in their minds (breakfast, an important meeting coming up, how to get the car fixed) that will have nothing to do with Moses. Again, as important as observation questions are, they cannot solve this problem easily.

In most studies the answers given to the approach questions are built on later. This is why it is especially important *not* to read the passage before the approach question is asked. The passage will tend to color the honest reactions people would otherwise give because they are of course *supposed* to think the way the Bible does. And they go along not facing the fact that they do not think the way the Bible does. Approach questions will not solve this difficult problem completely, but they are an attempt to help start.

Let me also mention a fifth and final type of question asked in these studies: feeling questions. These call for imaginative identification with characters. These will often elicit different responses from different people. There are no strict right or wrong answers to this type of question. Group members should be encouraged to see how others might have felt and discouraged from arguing about a right answer. The point is to help the passage come alive, to see it as a story about real people in a real setting.

As mentioned in the introduction, these studies are designed to be used in a sixty- to ninety-minute time slot. If your group is not used to spending this much time or doing homework between meetings, you may want to discuss ahead of time what will be needed. In any case, there are some suggestions at the end of the leader's notes for study 1 for discussing this issue.

If 60 to 90 minutes is impossible for your group, some options are still available. First, if everyone in the group has a copy of the guide and prepares before each meeting, discussion (especially of observation questions) will go much more quickly. Second, in each study some questions are preceded by an asterisk (*), indicating that this question can be skipped if you are pressed for time. Third, you can split a particularly long study in two. Studies 1, 3, 5, 7 and 8 will probably take the longest.

As you lead the study discussion itself, you will want to keep the following in mind:

☐ Do not answer your own question. If necessary, rephrase the question or ask, "Is the question clear?" Sometimes just repeating it will suffice. (The problem with answering your own questions is that discussion can be stifled if group members think the leader will do all the work for them, or if they are threatened because the leader "knows so much and I don't want to show how much I don't know.")

☐ Similarly, do not be afraid of silence. Give the group time to look for answers. Remember it took you time to find the answers too.

☐ Do not be content with just one answer. Try to get several people to contribute to the discussion. Ask, "What do the rest of you think?" Even observation questions often have more than one answer.

☐ Acknowledge all contributions. Never refuse any answer. If a wrong answer comes up, ask, "Which verse led you to that conclusion?" or again, "What do the rest of you think?"

☐ Likewise, do not be afraid of controversy. It can be very stimulating. If you do not resolve an issue completely, don't be frustrated. Move on and keep it in mind for later. A subsequent study might solve the problem.

☐ Stick to the passage under consideration. If someone insists on cross-referencing where it is not essential, suggest a poststudy discussion of the matter. Or try asking, "Which verse led you to that conclusion?"

☐ In the same way, stick to the topic under consideration. The questions will stimulate many ideas. Use the purposes at the beginning of each section in the leader's notes to guide you as to what is most relevant. But again be sensitive to the needs of individuals. Do not shut them off just for the sake of keeping a rule. Still, you might be able to deal with a person more openly after the study is over.

☐ Feel free to summarize, highlight background material (such as that found in the studies) or review past studies. But do not preach.

☐ Pray before, after, or before and after each study. Probably afterward would be the best time for group conversational prayer.

☐ Begin and end on time.

Many more suggestions and helps are found in James F. Nyquist's *Leading Bible Discussions* (IVP). Reading and studying through that would be well worth your time.

Study 1: Background and History

Purposes

☐ To establish a climate of openness in the group.

☐ To give opportunity for each person in the group to feel comfortable and listened to.

☐ To understand the biblical background of Moses and his times and to see a brief overview of the book of Exodus.

It is important that the first time your group meets you should spend most of your time getting acquainted, taking the first steps toward trusting one another. This may be new to the group if they are accustomed to starting right out with biblical content. But it will pay off significantly in the long run as you and your group increasingly identify with Moses and his pilgrimage toward greater intimacy with God. In this way God will meet you not only through Scripture but through that segment of the body of Christ which is your small group.

Following is a specific plan for this session which you may adapt to better fit the needs of your group.

Before Question 1. First, have everyone in the group tell his or her full name (including middle name) and then something about how he or she got the name. Each one can also give one or two personal facts (such as occupation, children or place of birth). You should go first so they will have a model. Keep things moving. Allow about one and one-half minutes per person.

Next, tell your group that the purpose of this first meeting is not merely to gain some biblical content but also to become better acquainted. For this reason, you think it would be good for you all to share something about why you are here. Begin by telling them why you chose this study. This may be as short as one sentence ("I have always wanted to know more about Moses' life") or as long as three minutes of sharing about how God has already spoken to you through the life of Moses. Then tell the group how you are feeling about leading the study, whether it be excited or apprehensive. The key is to be aware of your feelings and to be honest with the others. As you do this, you will be modeling openness and authenticity. This will set the tone for honest sharing throughout your sessions together. Usually, a group becomes only as vulnerable and honest as its leader.

Question 1. Now let each other person in your group tell why she or he is here. Having modeled the process, you can simply ask, "Why are *you* here?" and then expectantly look around the group. As people respond, don't be a passive listener! Allow your facial expression to illustrate that you are interested. Also ask a question here and there to clarify an answer. By your example, encourage others in the group to ask questions of the speaker also. This will help the group to become less leader centered.

Question 2. After giving everyone an opportunity to respond to these questions, take time to pray together. Help generate a sense of vitality in your prayers by first mentioning that the God who interacted with Moses thousands of years ago is the same God who is in the room with you today and that he is deeply concerned with every person. Encourage each person to talk openly with God about what he wants in each life throughout your weeks together. Again, you will be able to encourage others to the extent that God has met you, the leader, before the study.

Note: With a group of six people, you should have used about one-third of your allotted time for the study.

Question 3. Instead of reading the Genesis passages right away, try to draw from your group what they already know about the history of Israel. If the group has worked on the study ahead of time, you probably won't need to read the passages at all. If after drawing all you can from the group, some gaps remain in the discussion, have the passages read aloud which will fill in what's missing. (If you are running out of time, you can summarize briefly what is left unsaid.)

Then you read Genesis 50:22-26 and Exodus 1:1-7. (The reason for your reading this section is the hard-to-pronounce names!)

Also you might want to mention that *Israel* is another name for Jacob (see Gen 32:28).

Question 4. Have someone read the rest of Exodus 1 (vv. 8-22) and then discuss the questions.

Question 5. It is important that you, the leader, have the graph well in mind so that you can hold it up and *briefly* review it, pointing especially to the three high points. This quick overview will give your group security to see the big picture of where the drama is going.

Question 6. Take only about five minutes on just one of these four questions. Choose the one that flows best from the discussion.

Question 7. Explain that this question gives a head start on the next study as well as helping each other to know one another better. Tell your group that Moses had many different events and people in *his* life which made him what he became and that doing this exercise will help you to identify with him as you get into the future studies.

Read the example of the Christian chemistry professor. Now have the group take five minutes to jot down outstanding events and people they remember. (Come prepared with extra pencils and paper.)

While they do this, check to see how much time you have left. Roughly divide this time by the number of people you have in your group (not including yourself). This will give you an approximate idea of how long each person can talk. When the five minutes are up, let each person respond. You should wait until the beginning of the next session to tell about yourself.

Looking Ahead. Talk over the ground rules for your group. Would they like to make this a highly committed group? Could everyone make it a priority to be present each week? Could you agree to begin and end on time, taking an hour and a half for each session? Are you willing to prepare beforehand, filling out the answers in the book before coming to the group each week? The group must decide together exactly what will be expected of each member. You cannot impose your wishes. To the degree that you can agree, your group will derive maximum benefit from these studies.

Usually, people are eager to be challenged to high commitment. If some in the group do not wish to be as committed, accept that. Suggest that they would be more comfortable in a less highly committed group. It will be easier for them as well as prevent a watering down of the group as a whole if you can all be open about this at the first meeting.

Ask the members to write out the answers to study 2 for next week and to pray about what God will do in them through Exodus.

Study 2: Preparation for Service (Ex 1:22—3:1)

Purposes

☐ To be introduced to Moses.

☐ To see what God used in Moses' early years to prepare him for service.

☐ To take inventory of events in our lives which we consider both positive and negative as possible ways in which God may be preparing us for service.

☐ To consider one difficult area of my life and thank God for the way he will use it (or has already used it) to bring glory to himself through me.

Have you worked through the study questions? If not, please do not read further until you have done so.

Before Question 1. When the group got together for study 1, everyone except you shared the key people and events of his or her life. This time when your group meets, begin by sharing your own story. This should not take more than ten minutes. It should be as personal and authentic as you can make it. As your group observes your openness and willingness to reach out to them in trust, they will gradually begin to do the same. When you have finished, briefly tell (don't read) the introduction. It will serve as a bridge between your history-giving and the study. Either summarize yourself or ask a group member to summarize the events of chapter one and mention the fact that this all culminated with Pharaoh's action.

Questions 2-3. Have someone read aloud verses 1-11. While the story may be familiar to many, the point of these questions is to help you get underneath the well-known facts to see these characters as real people with real feelings. Notice too that God uses natural feelings, attitudes and circumstances to bring about his sovereign purposes. In this case, he used the natural compassion of an Egyptian woman for a baby and the natural love of a Hebrew mother for her child. Keep questioning your group until you get a full picture.

Question 4. Hebrew women often nursed their babies until the child was four years old. Also there may have been further contact with his mother (nurse) after he got into Pharaoh's daughter's house. Without this ancestral background, God's later revelation to Moses would have been rootless.

Question 5. Moses was doubtless reared with other princelings. He would have been trilingual at least (Hebrew, Egyptian, Midianite). Study of law would doubtless have been one aspect of any such education (Hammurabi's Code, for example, was widely studied and annotated by Egyptian scribes.) Moses would also have been subjected to the false gods of Egypt as well as to the temptations of a soft life.

Question 7. Try to get your group to feel this with Moses.

Question 8. Walt Kaiser has commented that Moses got his B.A. in political administration at Egypt Tech and his M.A. in desert survival at Midian Ag. School.

Question 10. Take time to let everyone read what they have written about Moses. If there are those who have not come up with a profile, encourage them to write it by next week. This could be used as an opportunity for you, the leader, to get to know those in your group better. Suggest your willingness to chat sometime during the week with those having trouble with the question. The rest of the studies will be far more meaningful if you gently but persistently encourage everyone to write a profile.

Questions 12-13. It is one thing to believe intellectually that God works through negative situations for good. It is quite another to absorb this into our own lives, especially while we are in the middle of a problem. If you have experienced such a situation recently or, more pertinently, if you happen to be in one right now, share this with your group. Remember that you as a leader do not have to see victories before God can use you. In fact, it may be that he will speak to the group through you even more powerfully when you are weak than when you have it all together. Your openness will help your group share their hurts.

Before the study ends, turn to next week's study and read the opening question. ("Have you ever had the feeling that God wanted you to do something that seemed beyond you?") Encourage the group members to think very practically and currently about this as they work through the study before your next meeting.

Study 3: The Prophet's Call (Ex 3:1—4:17)

Purposes

☐ To see how Moses responded to his call from God.

☐ To consider my response to God's call in my life.

If you have been touched by God through Scripture, your group will catch it and be more likely to respond also. This is particularly true of this study. Is there something going on in your life *right now* that you feel inadequate to handle? Did God speak through the passage and the study questions to help you deal with the problem? If so, can you share this with your group as you work through the study together? This is what will cause the Scriptures to spring alive! Be alert to others in the group who may have come prepared to share personally, also.

This is a long study. If your group does not have adequate time planned, you may need to divide the study, finishing it at your next gathering. This would be much better than rushing to finish it in one meeting.

Question 2. Don't be discouraged if people have trouble at first doing what this question asks. It takes imagination to identify with and see Moses as he walked along tending his sheep. If your group isn't used to doing this, it will take persistence on your part to draw them out. But the results are well worth the effort. Just keep on asking questions like, "What else does he hear?" "How old was he?" "Does he have a beard?" Your group will gradually catch on and do this sort of thing more easily the next time it comes up. And it will help Moses jump out of the page as a real person.

Question 5. The point of this question (which has been introduced by question 2) is to see that Moses needed to know that the God who spoke to him out of a bush far away from Palestine, where Abraham lives, and far away from Egypt, where the children of God now were, was nevertheless the same God who made a covenant with Abraham. See Genesis 15 and Exodus 2:24. Moses needs to know that God is personal, holy and trustworthy—the characteristics of the God of Abraham, Isaac and Jacob.

Question 8. Be sure to tell your group to keep their own call in mind as you go through this question. Allow anyone who wishes, to be specific about ways in which God spoke through the thoughts in this dialog between Moses and God. You, the leader, may need (and want) to do this first so that others can more easily risk being personal.

Question 10. Moses asked this question because he knew the Israelites would want to know the essential character of this God. Would this God be able to keep his promise? The name had to indicate that he would.

Question 11. " I AM WHO I AM." There is a future thrust in the core verb used here and brought out in the Revised Standard Version footnote to verse 14: "I WILL BE WHAT I WILL BE." This is similar to the sign given to Moses and indicates that who God is will be revealed as future events in Israel's history unfold. He will always be present, always acting, always participating in Israel's history; therefore, he will keep his promises of deliverance.

On a human level, we operate this way all the time: A girl meets a fellow and has a good first impression. But only as she gets to know him better will she be able to decide to marry him. She will watch his actions—how he treats others, whether he keeps his promises to her and so on. These actions will back up the fellow's words until the girl will see that he is who he says he is. In terms of who God is, it would be the experiences of the ten plagues, the parting of the Red Sea, survival in the wilderness and so on that would reveal his "name."

Question 12. Not only did God have to prepare Moses, he

had also to prepare Moses' audience, the Israelites and Pharaoh. The same with us. If our call involves speaking about God to others, he will need to prepare us and them. Our audience may not believe that we have something they want and need unless they see it in our lives.

Question 13. You and your group may not have had objective signs of any kind from God. If not, let this question rest. Or brainstorm what some of these signs might be. Some possibilities: a deep impression that a verse of Scripture is touching you in some important way, money that comes just when you need it and have been praying for it, a physical healing, circumstances which fit so perfectly that they cannot be accounted for apart from an answer to prayer.

Question 17. You will probably wish to discuss at this point the difference in the response of people to God's will. Do some in your group need more vigorous interaction with God than others before they do what God asks? Can people be at different stages in terms of needing to receive more reassurance or to obey immediately?

You may wish to read the last question in the study aloud without expecting an answer. Just let people think together quietly. Or there may be those who wish to respond. Give freedom for this, too.

Study 4: Failure and Discouragement (Ex 4:27—6:13)
Purposes

☐ To observe what Moses saw as failure following his call to service.

☐ To learn to trust God more fully during the adverse circumstances of our lives.

☐ To get in touch with some area of my life that is not going well and praise God for his sovereignty over that area.

Question 1. Be sure that you, the leader, never treat the opening question as rhetorical. You should always try to get in touch with something in your own life (the more current, the better) to which it applies. *Write down* your feelings toward God for this study. Be ready to share with your group if you need to. However, if you have modeled vulnerability so far in the group, you can be almost certain that others in the group will wish to share too. Ask them to do so before you get into the study itself. Then summarize (do not read) the brief background summary. Ask someone to read Exodus 4:27-31 aloud.

Questions 4-7. These are brief questions. Do not spend much time here.

Question 9. In essence, the answer you want here is God's character and covenant. Help your group to understand that what counts is who God *is* as he is revealed more and more to Moses and the Israelites. Note, too, that the covenant which he made with Abraham is "established" (6:4). It was still in force and God would now keep its terms.

Question 10. Help your group see the tenderness of the Lord. God was moved not only by the covenant but also by the wretched condition of his people. Note the tender expression, "I will take you for my people," in verse 7. If Pharaoh had only known the Israelites' true identity in God's sight!

Question 11. One of God's characteristics is that of redeemer. The word *redeem* in verse 6 refers to a member of a family buying back or ransoming another member of the family, especially when that member was in slavery for debt or about to go into slavery. Israel apparently had no earthly relative to redeem her, but God was now Israel's relative, her kinsman redeemer. This redemption was to be out of Egypt and into the Promised Land. Keep on asking for characteristics of God until you have quite a few. Be sure they are written down so that everyone can use them when you praise God together at the end of the study.

Questions 13-17. Encourage people to answer, but do not let the group get so bogged down that you do not get to the focus of the lesson found in questions 16 and 17. Be sure that you save plenty of time for praise. Center in on who God *is* rather than placing the emphasis on what he has *done* for you. The latter is more in the realm of thanksgiving and certainly has its place in the Christian life. But today, the emphasis should be on God's character.

Finally, remind everyone to prepare study 5 before your next meeting. Question 1 will take about thirty minutes—twenty to read the passage and ten to find the word *know*. The group should be encouraged to complete the rest of the study as well.

Study 5: Growth through Adversity (Ex 7:1—11:3)
Purposes
☐ To recognize God's greater purposes and plans for Israel, Egypt and Moses in the midst of suffering.
☐ To enlarge our concept of the sovereign God.
☐ To begin to see the difficult circumstances of my life as opportunities for bringing glory to God.
Question 1. If everyone prepared ahead of time, you will not need to read the entire passage aloud in the group.
Question 2. One of the most useful tools in studying the Bible inductively is the *law of repetition,* the reiteration of the same or similar terms. If you discover that a writer has used the same word or phrase over and over again, you can be quite sure that there is a point which he or she wishes to communicate. Such is the case in this passage in the author's use of the word *know.* You may wish to mention the law of repetition to your group and suggest that they use it as they study Scripture. It proves to be especially useful in this passage. Help your group to see how the repetition of the word *know* points the reader to the basic point God wanted to get across to Moses, the Israelites and the Egyptians.
Question 3. The answer to this question is basic for the understanding of question 4. Don't get bogged down in a discussion of God's sovereignty versus human free will. Perhaps you will want to mention that people have been arguing this question for centuries without coming to solid agreement and that

what you as a group need to know is that God was *using* natural circumstances and the character of Pharaoh for his purposes.

Question 9. It ought to be possible to praise God while in the middle of adversity rather than waiting until we see (in retrospect) the benefits which have come to us through the difficulty. Some things we learn once and for all (that two plus two equals four, for instance). But there are other things which have to be learned over and over. One of these is that when adversity hits us, our first question should be, "How can God use this for his glory?" Try to identify anything in your own life which has shown this to be true and share it with your group.

Study 6: Vindication and Victory (Ex 11:4—12:42)
Purposes

☐ To see God's purposes and plans at work as events culminate to free Israel and strengthen Moses.

☐ To focus on God's instructions for being released from the bondage of sin and think through how I would communicate these instructions to unbelievers.

The Passover feast was mainly an event commemorating the beginning of the Jewish nation and its deliverance from Egypt. It was not until many years later that the event took on a deeper significance—the paschal lamb of Christ whose life was given as a substitute for ours. The main point to emphasize in this study is not the symbolism of the various parts of the Passover feast but rather the importance of Moses' and the Israelites' faithful obedience to God's plan for redemption from the bondage of Egypt.

Likewise to participate in the salvation from sin that God offers, we must come in the way God has set rather than in some way of our own choosing. It is through the foolishness of the cross (1 Cor 1:18) that we see God's power to deliver us from the bondage and penalty of sin.

Question 1. The maidservant who is behind the mill (11:5) is an Egyptian phrase for the "poorest of the poor."

Question 2. Leaven is like yeast. To make unleavened bread

(12:8), it is not necessary to give it time to rise. We might call it a quick bread. Thus unleavened bread is the bread of one who is ready to be obedient at a moment's notice. To leaven one's bread was to risk not being ready when the word to march came, hence a sign of unbelief.

Study 7: Leadership under Duress (Ex 14:1—15:21)
Purposes
☐ To consider the drama in an episode of Moses' mission.
☐ To see God acting in history and to praise him for his power, faithfulness and steadfast love to both the Israelites and to all people who belong to him.
☐ To spend time praising God for his actions of power and love in my own life and for specific attributes of his character.

To the degree that you, the leader, have been caught up in the wonder and drama of this magnificent passage will your group be captivated also. Have you made questions 12 and 13 personal this week? Don't try to lead this study until you have done so!

Question 3. This question and others which ask what you will do with specific persons in each scene are meant to be guidelines for your own elaborations. You may think of others that will guide your group into getting into the feel of the passage. Be sure that your group gets specific about how they will set the scenes. For instance, for question 3a, don't stop with an answer like, "They would be terrified." Rather, get answers like, "Some of the people would be unable to move as they looked toward the Egyptians. Others would be rushing to Moses and crying for help. Husbands would have their arms around their wives in some cases. Mothers would be trying to comfort children. Some would be praying. Facial expressions would be of abject terror and, in some cases, of anger toward Moses. Maybe somebody would be shaking his fist at Moses."

Question 6. Not only will the hearts of the Egyptians be hardened so that they will follow them into the sea, but God will also be glorified. Be sure both aspects come out in your discussion.

Question 11. Recall that the name of God can well be translated, "I will be what I will be." Only in his subsequent *actions* would he be known to Israel.

Question 12. Think of a creative way to have your group read this passage. You may want to have different pairs or trios of people in your group read each paragraph. Reading in unison could give greater feel for the entire people of Israel as they sing praise to God. Encourage the group to read with gusto, just as the people sang. (Be sure those reading together are reading the same translation!)

Another way would be to use a narrator who would read verses 1-3; then part of the group would respond with verse 4 and the other part with verse 5, alternating until they come to verse 11 when the narrator reads again. One group would read verse 12, the narrator would read verse 13 and then the two groups would again read alternate verses to the end of verse 18.

Questions 12-13. You may wish to mention the strong emphasis on God's steadfast love—a characteristic that some critics of the Old Testament feel is present only in the New Testament. Be sure to use the attributes you have found in the passage as you spend time praising God even though you may draw from your own store of knowledge to praise God for other characteristics of his.

Study 8: Life in Relationship (Ex 19:1—20:20)

Purposes

☐ To see how God established a spiritual relationship with Israel as a nation and gave principles on which that relationship could be maintained.

☐ To understnd how, in Christ, this relationship has become individual and internal.

☐ To show how this life in relationship with God is the chief catalyst to holiness.

☐ To cause me to judge everything I do and think in the coming week by the standard of whether or not this action or thought will please the God I love.

Almost everyone has some familiarity with the Ten Commandments. The purpose of this study is to lift the decalogue out of the realm of a well-known set of rules into the category of guidelines whereby human beings can please the One who loves them and has redeemed them. This session with your group will be greatly enhanced if you can authentically share a recent example from your own life in question 1.

Question 1. If the group has examples to share, you may want to keep your example until question 15.

Question 6. "Israel never thought of Yahweh as living on Sinai, but only as appearing there. Many other places were equally associated with divine manifestations in patriarchal days (e.g. Bethel, Gn 28)." R. Alan Cole, *Exodus,* p. 146. The point of this question is to show that Yahweh, unlike the gods of other religions, took the initiative. The Shepherd finds the sheep, not the other way around.

Question 11. In addition to various practical answers to this question, try to get your group to see that one of the more profound observations is that salvation precedes sanctification. (The Israelites were freed from Egypt by God to be his chosen people before they were given God's prescription for right living as summarized in the Ten Commandments.)

Question 17. It is vital that your group become concrete on this question. Brainstorm some ways in which people can and do try to dodge God in their thought, life and actions. This can be general but should serve to stir up the group's thinking about possibilities. If someone wishes to share personally and specifically, be sure to fully accept him or her without giving advice or suggestions.

Study 9: Moses the Mediator (Ex 24)

Purposes

☐ To observe the ratification ceremony of the Mosaic covenant.

☐ To understand how Christians today have a fuller realization of God under the new covenant than the old.

☐ To thank God for the blessings which are mine under the new covenant.

Question 1. Nadab and Abihu are the two sons of Aaron, whose death, under God's judgment, is recorded in Numbers 3:4; the actual story is in Leviticus. This explains their failure to reappear later. It also assures us of the authenticity of the tradition, for no one would have inserted their names here in the account of such an important event. *Seventy* in "Seventy of the elders" is an approximate number, representing either the twelve tribes of Israel or Jacob's seventy descendants (Num 11:16; Lk 10:1)—Cole, *Exodus,* p. 184.

Questions 5-6. One purpose of these two questions is to establish background for the study which is to follow. Don't spend much time on them. Merely establish that God was indeed making provision for the people while Moses was taken from them.

Questions 8-14. These questions which deal with the new covenant can lead to exciting discussion. Since some members of your group may not be familiar with the relationship between the two covenants, you may find the following quote from R. K. Harrison useful: "When the new covenant was inaugurated by the atoning work of Jesus Christ on Calvary, the important development of personal, as opposed to corporate faith and spirituality, was made real for the whole of mankind. Henceforward anyone who submitted himself consciously in faith to the person of Christ as Saviour and Lord could claim and receive membership in the church of God. The new covenant in the blood of Christ, therefore, is the fruition of God's sovereign grace, conveying through a specifically spiritual relationship an adequate provision for the forgiveness of all sin, a more profound experience of divine mercy as a result of such forgiveness and a wider sense of brotherhood among men by virtue of membership in the fellowship of Christ" (Harrison, *Jeremiah,* p. 140).

Study 10: Fall and Restoration (Ex 32)

Purposes

☐ To see how the Israelites broke loose from God's authority.

☐ To learn how we can avoid spiritual pitfalls.

☐ To cause me to meet faithfully with God each day in order to guard the reality of the invisible God in my own life, to intercede for the growth and purity of other Christians, and to intercede for the universal church, that its witness will be untarnished.

Alan Cole says, "This is a very vivid passage, showing that the spiritual experience of Moses was not shared by his people. Even Aaron comes out badly; but he had neither had the vision at Sinai as a shepherd, nor had he had the unique preparation in Egypt that Moses had had. But even Israel we must not judge too harshly; they were a slave people, still with the minds of slaves, even if God had set them free. Paul makes the same complaint about Christians in Galatians 5:1. Indeed, much of his language in describing them seems drawn from the descriptions of erring Israel in the Old Testament. It is because Israel is so like us in every way that the stories of Israel have such exemplary value (1 Cor. 10)"—Cole, *Exodus,* p. 212.

Question 4. "To use any image as symbolic of God is misleading (Ex 20:23). To use a bull as symbol of God is worse; further, it is blasphemy if the 'new' god is called Yahweh, as apparently it was on this occasion. In addition, verse 6 seems to show all the licentious Baal worship of Canaan (cf. Num. 25:1-9)."— Cole, *Exodus,* pp. 214-15.

Question 6. Cole says that in verse 10 is "a real temptation to Moses (as real as the temptations of the Lord), or it would have lost its whole meaning. It was the fulfillment of God's promises to Abraham (Gn. 12:2) and to Jacob (Gn. 35:11), but the people would now bear the tribal name of 'sons of Moses', not 'sons of Israel'. The price was only to abandon his shepherd's calling and to let Israel go. Their own behaviour had earned their rejection, as he is reminded here. But no true shepherd could do this: so comes the intercessory prayer of Moses (verses 11-13) taken up again in verses 31, 32"—Cole, *Exodus,* p. 217.

Regarding "the LORD *repented,*" Cole says, "The meaning is not that God changed His mind; still less that He regretted something that He had intended to do. It means, in biblical language, that He now embarked on a different course of action from that already suggested as a possibility, owing to some new factor which is usually mentioned in the context. We are not to think of Moses as altering God's purpose towards Israel by this prayer, but as carrying it out: Moses was never more like God than in such moments, for he shared God's mind and loving purpose" —Cole, *Exodus,* p. 217.

Question 7. You may not need to ask the last two questions here if the first one ("What was Moses' response?") brings out a full answer.

Question 8. "Compare Josiah's treatment of the altar (and bull?) of Bethel (II Kings 23:15). Such treatment of the golden bull is symbolic, repudiating its claim (stated by its followers, Ex. 32:4) to be the one who had led Israel out of Egypt. In addition, it is the treatment of Canaanite gods demanded by the covenant terms (Ex. 23:24)"—Cole, *Exodus,* pp. 218-19.

Study 11: "Show Me Thy Glory" (Ex 33)

Purposes

☐ To note Moses' deep concern for Israel and for his own personal encounter with God.

☐ To see that God delights in persistent prayer for his presence in our lives individually and corporately.

☐ To desire to know God to such a degree that I, like Moses, will persist with him in prayer until he reveals himself to me more deeply.

To many people, debating with God in prayer displays incredible arrogance and lack of spirituality. Rather it requires a great deal of steadfastness and spiritual maturity. You, as leader, will be more effective in this study if you have struggled with God yourself. If you have not, share this with your group and learn from this passage together.

Study 12: God's Shining Witness (Ex 34)
Purposes

☐ To observe the effect on Moses as he personally encountered the God this chapter portrays.

☐ To observe the effect which Moses' deeper relationship with God produced on the Israelites.

☐ To understand that if I, like Moses, encounter the greatness of God in a deep way, that this will be a powerful witness to those around me (whether I am aware of it or not).

It would be good if your group could agree to keep this session open ended so that you will not be restricted by having to finish at a certain time. The questions at the end of the study are very pesonal and could be far-reaching in their implications for group members. Thus, it is important to consider them unhurriedly.

Be sure to let everyone in the group tell what the Lord has shown them during the studies. It would also be good if the group took time to pray for everyone individually before you finish. You may wish to do this, mentioning each person by name. Or, as two or three people share at the end, stop and have several pray for them. Then move on to let two or three others share and pray again until everyone has been covered.